Th
Oratory of Light

Other books by James Harpur

Poetry

The Examined Life, Two Rivers Press, Reading, 2021
The White Silhouette, Carcanet, Manchester, 2018
Angels and Harvesters, Anvil Press, London, 2012
The Dark Age, Anvil Press Poetry, London, 2007
The Gospel of Joseph of Arimathea, Wild Goose Publications,
Glasgow, 2007
Oracle Bones, Anvil Press Poetry, London, 2001
The Monk's Dream, Anvil Press Poetry, London, 1996
A Vision of Comets, Anvil Press Poetry, London, 1993

Translation

*Fortune's Prisoner: The Poems of Boethius's Consolation of
Philosophy*, Anvil Press, 2007

Novel

The Pathless Country, Cinnamon Press, Cardiff, 2021

Non-Fiction

The Pilgrim Journey, Lion Books, London, 2016
Love Burning in the Soul: The Story of the Christian Mystics,
Shambhala, Berkeley, Ca., 2005

The Oratory of Light

Poems in the spirit of St Columba

James Harpur

wild goose
publications

www.**ionabooks**.com

First published 2021 by
Wild Goose Publications
Suite 9, Fairfield
1048 Govan Road, Glasgow G51 4XS, Scotland
the publishing division of the Iona Community.
Scottish Charity No. SC003794. Limited Company Reg. No. SC096243.

ISBN 978-1-84952-790-3

Cover image and internal images © Paul Ó Colmáin

The publishers gratefully acknowledge the support of the Drummond Trust,
3 Pitt Terrace, Stirling FK8 2EY in producing this book.

Overseas distribution
Australia: Willow Connection Pty Ltd, Unit 4A, 3–9 Kenneth Road,
Manly Vale, NSW 2093
New Zealand: Pleroma, Higginson Street, Otane 4170, Central Hawkes Bay

Printed by Bell & Bain, Thornliebank, Glasgow

Contents

Part Three: Waiting for the Angels

Preface

Be kind to one another. That's all there is to life.
Be at peace.

St Columba

I began writing this book during the Covid pandemic, when the enforced physical restrictions at home took me off to the imaginative freedom of the island of Iona. I still remember my first visit there and how the boat across the narrow sound from Mull delivered me to what seemed like the Otherworld – what George MacLeod, the founder of the Iona Community, described as 'a "thin place" – only a tissue paper separating the material from the spiritual'.

Each poem in this book has grown from the seeds of reported words or deeds of St Columba (or Columcille, 'dove of the church'), especially those found in the works of Adomnán (d. 704), Columba's first biographer, and Manus O'Donnell (d. 1564). In most cases poetic thoughts and images would emerge from this material and I would try to follow them (sometimes in the persona of a Columban monk) to see where they would lead me, hoping to arrive at a place that would have been congenial to Columba himself. I have also included some versions of anonymous medieval Irish poems ascribed to the authorship of the saint. I have added 'After the Irish' to distinguish these from the others, and have noted all the literary sources at the back of the book.

Historians remind us that Columba was as much a tough, worldly power-broker as a 'saintly' spiritual leader and tend to disassociate him from accounts of his miracles. But it isn't necessary to believe or disbelieve in the miracles associated with Columba to see that they betoken a world view in which the mysteries of the universe – which might include clairvoyance, visions and dreams, spiritual healing and synchronistic encounters – are to be valued, marvelled at, explored and celebrated; a world view that posited a God-centred universe in which everything – people, animals, angels and the elements – had its place and was subject to divine laws and susceptible to the power of prayer. This type of world view has also been the hallmark of the oldest streams of poetry, which is itself dedicated to exploring the inexhaustible realm of the Imagination. As William Blake said, 'the history of all times and places is nothing else but improbabilities and impossibilities'.

James Harpur, West Cork, 2021

Iona Sound

You look for signs for why you're here
And try to settle on the sun's confetti
Aglitter on the aisle of the water
Unrippling in white towards the shore –

As if God's unveiling a truth, a path
That, like a bridegroom, only you can sense.
Waves break randomly on the vessel;
Or do they press you to your destiny?

Glimpses of the distant ocean shimmer
In the way that endlessness shimmers;
And as the wind divests your self of self
You wonder what on earth a boundary is!

Above the abbey tower doves fly up –
White petals from a rose, or notes of a song
Configuring a pattern that attunes your soul
To what it now remembers it has lost.

Exile

Eithne's Carol

(Before the birth of Columba, 7 December, 521)

One night, my son inside me still,
The fields of Gartan deep in frost,
When star on star was gathering
To light a candle for the Christ

I saw a shape within the fire –
A golden angel who revealed
A mantle woven with the colours
Of all the flowers of the fields.

And how I cried when suddenly
The angel cast it into space –
I watched the cloak unfold and cover
A swathe of mountains, plains and seas

And heard a whispering: 'Your son
Shall mirror the flowers of this world.
He'll be a prophet to his people,
Exuding the fragrance of the Lord.'

That night, my son inside me still,
The fields of Gartan deep in frost
When star on star was gathering
To light a candle for the Christ

I thought how Life expands from flesh
And how the spirit would unfurl
My son and clothe the world with light –
My son so tightly, darkly curled.

On Leaving Ireland

The seagulls heckling Lough Foyle
　　Are full of farewell cries –
But cannot join my coracle
　　And its wake of sad goodbyes.

(After the Irish)

Retrospect

This ash-grey
   Eye
That sends its gaze
To Ireland
Will never linger
Upon her men
Or women
Again.

(After the Irish)

Exile

A place where Ireland is invisible –
The verdict was the lodestar of my will
Drawing along the foaming coracle

For I knew I'd be distracted from the Lord
If my heart's eye from every cliff or hill
Migrated back to Derry, Donegal.

Then landfall on that sunny grainy day –
Iona, fireflies of drizzle, *tabula rasa*!

But Satan must have been a stowaway.

I drowned myself in books and catching fish,
In songs and fasts but still the dreams increased,
My soul reviving what my mind had crushed:

Unable to see home the more I saw
The hounding fields of Derry, Donegal.

Nostos

Lord, in dream I cross
The vast grey ocean
Rolling through waves and troughs
To sweetest Ireland.

And as my boat arrives
The seagulls scream
Their welcome in the skies,
Rejoicing that I'm home.

Gliding on Lough Foyle
With swans to serenade me
At last I find my soul
On Mount Binevenagh.

By the abbey of Durrow
The elms are whispering …
And in the startle of a flurry
A blackbird sings.

At dawn in Ross Grencha
I hear the stags; and cuckoos
At the tremble of summer
Blow echoes through the woods.

(After the Irish)

Islands

What's better than being on an island
  And gazing out to sea
As waves crash and coalesce and crest
  And roar their hymns to God?

To see the wave-rilled sand
  And hear the cry of birds.
To listen to shingle-shush or by the graveyard
  The ocean's steady beat.

To watch the patterns of the gulls
  In speckles in the sky;
And spot the wonder that's the whale
  Climbing from the sea.

To contemplate the tides, and my secret name:
  'Cul ri Erin',
'The man who turned his back on Ireland',
  (And who recalls her every day).

(After the Irish)

Bountiful

The West is full of apple-trees –
As well as princes, kings, galore!
The sloes are plentiful and juicy
And fruits bejewel the forest floor.

(After the Irish)

To Live in Derry

If I possessed the whole of Alba –
　From boundary to boundary　–
I'd swap it for a single hut
　In the heart of lovely Derry.

(After the Irish)

The Oaks of Derry

I love Derry for its peace
   And all its purity;
And for the angels on each leaf
   Of every oak tree.

(After the Irish)

Nine Waves

So many angels spread across
　The Derry fields and hills they moved
Offshore to make another home.

For a distance of nine waves
　They rose like golden seahorses
Above the rolling silvery foam.

The Worst Fear

The
Prospect
Of death, hellfire,
Instils a trembling fear
Inside me.
But more than these:
The sound
Of axe
On trees
In
Derry.

(After the Irish)

The Mayhem of Miracles

Wings

When he was singing in the chapel
  His voice would float across Iona
And harvesters could hear each syllable.

Yet we, his brothers in the choir, knew
  His voice to be no louder than our own
And that the spirit took his song, and flew.

The Skull

'Once when Columba was walking by the River Boyne,
a giant skull of a man was sent to him.'

The death's head fixed him
With eyes of two small caves.
Columba wondered who he was
    And kneeled to pray.

And through the power of the Lord
The skull began to speak:
'I am Cormac, your ancestor –
    My faith was weak.

But God predicted that one day
You would discover me.
Now pray for my soul and let me rise
    To eternity.'

Columba prayed and straightaway
A spirit flew to the sky
While on the ground the skull relaxed
    Its rictus smile.

Vision

At certain times   my soul   unpeels itself
And I see the darkness   thinning
And I feel a lightness   lightening
And I can see   the universe –
This world   the flash of grass
A sudden swaying   residues of green;
At night   the great furnace
Flinging sparks   across the dark –
Too vast for waking comprehension …
Then all draws tight
Into
a
single
blade
of
light.

Columba the Scribe

My fingers ache from writing –
   My feather's beak
   Scratch-squeaks
Its beetle-gleaming liquid –
The rhythm of my quill
   Lets pages drink
   Wisdom in an ink
Extracted from green holly –
On countless fields of vellum
   My flagging pen
   Imprints without end
A track for bookish pilgrims.

(After the Irish)

The Oratory of Light

Too dark for copying a book
And yet Columba was at work –

His window frame a glowing sheet
Because above his manuscript

His feather-nimble fingers glowed
Like fiery buds of candle gold.

The Missing Vowel

(Columba to Baithéne, having been asked by the latter to have his copy of a psalter checked)

'You doubt your talent as a scribe?
Your work, I did predict,
Would be pristine except there'd be
   a missing I in it.

Your brothers scrutinised the script
and finally found the place
in which you should have put an I
   but actually left a space.

Baithéne, there was a moment when
You were so rapt and still
that God replaced your mortal I
   with his eternal will.'

Spilled Ink

Inside his hut
The saint predicted:
'A visitor
Will come today
To see me here
And spill my ink.'
So I, Diormit,
Stood guard
Outside the door
Alert to stop
This visitor
From rushing in.
I must admit
I left my post
For just a bit …
But time enough:
The visitor
Arrived, burst in –
So keen to kiss
Columba's hand
His habit flicked
The inkhorn
Spilled the ink.
Love, I think,
Can't wait –
Must have its fill:
Its way is joy
And ink will spill.

The Visitor

A crane arrived, crumpled in the waves,
Pulled back and sloshed towards the shore,
A dimming heart, a mess of feathers.

We witnessed how he fed it back to life;
Until the bird would trail him everywhere –
In chapel it would kneel by his side.

'This crane will rise up on the third day
Returning to its home in Ireland;
But we must use our spirit wings and pray
For glimpses of our heavenly abode.'

The third day, we assembled on the strand
And watched the bird unfold above the ocean,
Diminish to a freckle on the skies

Leaving a silver feather in our minds.

Ballad of the Milk Vessel

One day I saw him bless a churn
   A boy had on his back –
It lurched like someone being sick,
   Vibrated hard – then crack! –

Its straps broke and down it crashed,
   The milk glugged out in streams –
A devil fled with a screech of a curse,
   The boy let out a scream.

Columba said: 'Give all to God.
   Each vessel must be blessed:
For Satan may turn a harmless pot
   Into a demon's nest.'

Since then I keep on checking pails
   I'm lugging from the well –
Afraid I'll see a fiend who winks
   His pebble eye of hell.

The Creature in the River Ness

'The switch between the calm of life
And its disturbance – an accident, a death –
Can take a second: once, a monk of mine
Dived off our coracle to swim to shore
When from the smoothing river a rock
Flew up – a head, two eyes and jaws
Fenced with fangs like walrus tusks –
The river seemed to part to let it through –
This evil soul-destroyer! – I prayed –
My heart in plunges of panic –
For God to strike the monster but …
I felt my arm rise up   my fingers make
The sign of the cross   and phrases
like sweet breath   issued from my mouth.
The beast recoiled   before a gale of grace
And slipped below   the surface of the water
So easily   a ripple brushed the Ness
Like a lover's absentminded caress.'

Psalm 44

Outside the slab ramparts of King Brude
We chanted like Jericho warriors:
We have heard with our ears, O God …

The druids shrieked to shatter our psalm –
But made the spirit give Columba's voice
The sound of waves on cliffs – a distant boom –

Crows took flight as though before thunder –
We have heard with our ears, O God,
How you drove the heathen with your hand –

And fishes in the nearby Ness scattered –
We saw the king clench his pulsing head
To block our incantation to the Lord

To drive away the heathen with his hand
And make a mumbling realm a singing land.

The Healing Stone

He threw the white stone in the water –
We held our breath
Afraid that if we let it out
We might affect the balance of fate –

And watched King Brude grapple
With whisperings only he could hear:
The spectre of '*One God*', '*healing*' and worse,
The mayhem of a miracle.

O how relieved he was to see it sink –
How quick to scream a curse

When it bobbed up like an apple.

Ballad of the Spring

Columba was in Ardnamurchan
  Among the surly Picts,
A craggy barren spit of land
  With wave-gouged cliffs.

A mother came and thrust her child
  To be baptised by him;
But the land was far too stony and dry
  Without a well or stream.

Columba shut his eyes and prayed
  Then blessed a nearby rock –
And straightaway there splutter-gushed
  A fountain from a crack.

Everybody was struck dumb
  By the spray of holy water –
The woman could not strike a word
  But handed him her daughter.

He sprinkled droplets on the child
  And raised her to the skies;
Then from the silence seagulls loosed
  A thousand new-born cries.

The Falling Monk

'Angelic time is always in the present
And has no barriers of land or sea;
And angels always shadow us … unless
Our sins create a deafness in them.
At prayer one day I saw a vision
Of Durrow, a thousand miles away –
A roof, a monk with straw – he slipped –
I saw him plummeting and prayed
With such urgency the words came out
As "Help! Help! Help!"
                  Immediately
The angel by my side flew off –
I saw the monk still falling through the air
And then a glimmering below him –
Somehow he was arrested in his flight,
Suspended just above the ground
By arms the glow of ripened corn
That held him like a child, just born.'

Columba on the Island of Hinba

Three days he had no food or water!
Something had to give inside that cell.
We pictured him prostrate in prayer –

Yet more than prayer it must have been;
More like a vision of God … or angels:
For soon a light suffused his oratory –

The day concealing what the darkness lit –
The windows glowing softly as an aura.

And then it happened on the third night:

The door cracks of his cell shone
And on the facing wall we saw
A ray – as if of purest morning sun –

Imprint a keyhole shape in gold

Through which we spied the kingdom of the Lord.

The Bread of Light

One time when visiting
The crust of Hinba island

St Brendan watched Columba
Blessing the bread in chapel –

A ball of fire like a comet
Hovered above his head –

The glittery particles
Sift-shifting to a column

Rose and rose to heaven

From the fountain of the bread.

Defending the Poets

(Columba to King Aed at the council of Druim Cett in Derry.)

'If you think poems are just *fables*
Then why not food and … clothing, too?
The entire world might be a fable
  Including me and you!

Faced with fables I would choose
The one most likely to survive:
Colours blacken in the grave
  But poetry stays alive.

When God put people on this earth
Beginning with Adam and Eve
He gave each one a worldly craft
  Or gift of purity.

Wheelwrights and smiths have art
But also poets with their rhymes.
The grace of making poetry
  Is the greatest gift of time.'

(After the Irish)

The Pattern of the Day

'You ask me how I spend my day?
I wake and grant my time to God
And he informs my head and heart.
I'd say to you don't think, but *do*.
Allow the spirit to guide your hand
And soften your speech; live life
As if you're on the verge of singing;
Above all, carry out simple tasks
With love. That's the hardest thing.

There is a time for breaking bread.
A time for walking on the shore.
A time for picking seaweed off the rocks.
A time for fishing for the brethren.
A time for giving food out to the poor.
A time for praying to the Lord.
A time for sleeping in your bed;
That's all, that's all.'

The Whale

'Last night, at midnight, a great whale arose
from the depth of the sea ...'
Columba's warning to Baithéne.

We sailed with Baithéne from Iona
Towards the island of Tiree
When gazing at the white horizon
We caught a movement in the sea –

A mound emerging from the waves
And heading for our coracle –
Foam-water streaming from its head
Between the studs of barnacles –

We shrank ourselves, prayed aloud,
Beseeched Columba for protection –
But Baithéne cried: 'This beast's like us!
We *all* belong to God's creation.'

He blessed the sea, he blessed the whale
Who duly dived below the surface ...
A shadow passed beneath our boat

And the hole in the ocean healed itself.

Song of the Contrary Winds

Two men were sailing on a certain day:
Colman south to Ireland
Baithéne northwards to Tiree.
  The wind could not obey both men that day.

They went along and asked the saint to pray:
Colman for a northern wind
Baithéne for a southern breeze.
  The wind could not obey both men that day.

And on that certain day Columba prayed:
Baithéne crossed the sea
The wind behind his sails
  And sped towards the island of Tiree.

And later on that day Columba prayed:
The wind wheeled about
And Colman duly sailed
  And made his way to Ireland, heading south.

Two men were sailing on a certain day:
Colman south to Ireland
Baithéne north towards Tiree –
  And the wind obeyed the saint that blessèd day.

Abbot Cainnech's Shoe

The ocean herding waves like whales
Our vessel spun in a whirlpool –
Us begging him to stop the wind –
Him bellowing he could not pray
But Cainnech, yes, *Cainnech,* would –
Yet he was a thousand miles away!

In the refectory of Aghaboe

The abbot heard Columba's cry –
Dropped everything and left a shoe
In running off to pray in chapel.

Then as the wind became a sigh
Columba saw a vision of a table:
And there, below, a shoe marooned –

A tiny currach, a sea of stone.

Baitan's Grave

'You will be buried in a grave on which
a woman will drive her sheep.'
Columba to Baitan.

In the desert of the ocean
A pilgrim seeking peace
Among the thud of waves
Baitan cannot believe
That in this realm of whales,
A liquid world configuring
Itself anew each moment,
Columba's prophecy
Can ever come to pass.
And even when the angels
Lead him back to Ireland
To what in time will be
His bed of resurrection,
The oak grove of Galgach;
No inkling of the prophecy
Before his final breath ...

But then there comes that day,
A feud between two tribes –
A flight of refugees
A woman driving sheep
Across a soft-soiled grave
Where hooves thud out a smile
On Baitan's brightening face.

O Apple Tree

On the south side of the monastery
Of the Oakwood Plain, your roots
Forsook sweet earth and you brought forth
  A crop of sour fruits.

But then Columba came, late harvest,
And watched your branches sway –
He blessed your hanging globes of apples,
  Which sweetened straightaway.

Who knows when he will come to us –
We might be walking on a road
Or working in the fields – the stranger
  Who lightens us with words

Or gives the blessing of a smile
That penetrates our core
And makes our hearts fill up with love,
  Ripening once more.

The Door

The church at Tirdaglas
By the meadow of the two streams
Was locked
And no one had the keys.
'The Lord,' Columba said,
'Can't be shut out.
He *is* the door.' Whereupon
He knocked.
A silence, then we heard
A bolt drawn back;
With fingertips he pressed –
The door opened wide.
In shock
We stood around
Half fearing we might see
God inside.
Then as he ventured in
The miracle occurred:
I felt door on door opening
In mind –
Or soul or heart or body –

And moving to an 'apse' of light
I saw
As from reflections of the streams
The dazzle of two suns
Which made a nothing of everything –
'Key' and 'lock' were meaningless
For I was passing through
Myself
And 'I' and 'door' were one.

Ballad of the Book of Glass

One night while resident on Hinba
   Columba saw a vision –
An angel held a book of glass
   On which the Lord had written:

'You must ensure the man called Aedan
   Becomes Dalríada's king!'
But wary of this man, our brother
   Refused to give his blessing.

And I say that for each of us there is a book of glass.

The angel put the book aside
   And lashed him with a whip;
Next day Columba touched his back
   And felt a fiery stripe.

That night the angel reappeared
　　The book within his clasp –
Again Columba bit his lip
　　And cringed before the lash.

And I say that for each of us there is a book of glass.

Then on the third night he relented
　　And proffered his consent;
So the angel left a God-blessed king
　　And a dog-whipped saint.

And I say that for each of us there is a book of glass:
And if we disobey God's script, we'll count the cost in scars.

Waiting for the Angels

Harvest Spirit

Returning home at sunset,
  A day of waspy fields,
We came to a sudden halt
  Because we felt such ease,
Infusing joy, as if ...
  We'd stepped into paradise.

Next day it was the same
  And Baithéne said to us:
'Who senses something strange?'
  I said, 'I smell a fragrance
Of herbs, wild flowers –
  And look, such radiance!'

The others all agreed
  And Baithéne made us sit:
'Columba knows we're weary.
  Each evening to refresh us
He sends the holy spirit
  To meet us at this place.'

We felt a holy silence
  dismiss our puzzling,
A coolness brush our faces –
  A breeze had stirred
As from the hovering
  Of a great invisible bird.

Valediction of the Reptiles

I remember that day in summer,
The summer he left this earth,
We were labouring in the fields,
The sunfall side of the island,
When he appeared in a cart.
We dropped our tools, expecting him
To tell us news; a guest arriving,
Or a point of discipline perhaps.
He stood above us on a mound
And raised his palms: 'Dear brothers,
This is the last time I shall come
To see you harvesting the fields.
My time is near.'
                  The wind had dropped.
All we could hear was the sea
Beating itself against the rocks.
We bowed our heads and kneeled.
In the tremble of the silence he said:
'Listen: I'll soon be going home
But leave this island with a blessing.
Creatures that creep along on bellies
Shall not harm cattle or people.'

As he pronounced this prophecy
We heard the strangest rustling,
A whispering like a liturgy

In thistles, furze, long grass –
As if Iona's snakes and lizards
Were hissing their farewells to him
Before slithering into the past.

On the Shore

One day I saw him lying on the sand
And saw the pious toll upon his bones:

The wind got up and smoothed his robe
Pressing out the ladder of his ribs.

Dies Irae

Not long before he passed away
I found him working in the corn mill;
And as he ground the grain
His eyes were flickering, filled
With light and distance –
His lips muttering, fingers tapping
A strange unearthly beat;
And as I stood there wondering
Whether I should stay or leave
I heard him repeat:
'*Dies irae, dies irae* …
The day of the righteous king!
The day of the lord is coming –
Dies irae
Day of vengeance and of anger,
Of darkness and miasma;
Day of shocking wonders
Day of shattering thunder
Dies irae
Day of tightening fear,
Of bitterness and tears
When women's love will cease,
Desire gives way to peace,
When urge to fight has flown
And lust for the world has gone.'

The Receiving Angels

'You wonder why I mourn this day
That marks my thirty years of exile?
I've prayed to God to free my soul
From flesh for such a while …

And then, at last, the day arrived –
I looked up, saw his kingdom open –
A waterfall of angels
Streaming down to take me home!

They never reached Iona …

But ranged along the shore of Mull –
Impeded by the prayers of strangers
Begging God to keep me well.

Each day I grieve to see the angels
Across the Sound, singing hymns –
My ember soul waiting to flare
From the wind-rush of their wings.'

The Gift

Six days before his soul departed
He was in chapel taking Eucharist;
And at the breaking of the bread
We saw him falter, raise his eyes –
As if the sun had eased through mist
And cast its glory on his face.

He later said he'd seen an angel there
Composed of something glittering,
'A figure shaped from golden air'
Who told him 'God desired a present'.

How could almighty God want anything!
Six days we bickered over what was meant
Until our father died …
                  when I confessed
God's gift was like the Devil's theft.

The White Horse

I won't forget that evening: the path
Which seemed to lead anywhere but home;
The way he just sat down, out of breath.

A horse – the one that carried vessels for us –
Came trotting along and halted,
began nuzzling our brother's chest.

Its eyes blinking, full of tears –
I stared in wonder. Cradling its head
Columba whispered soothing words.

I said: 'This animal's delaying us.
Our time's precious.' He replied: 'Diarmaid,
He's just divined the day of my death.

He cannot speak, so let him weep –
Our brother animals have foresight;
He's simply saying farewell to me.'

At last he gave his blessing to the horse,
Who sloped away. I helped him up,
Held his arm and we resumed the path

Each step now falling like a heartbeat –
I willed the sinking sun to stop.
To stop the sadness galloping towards me.

Transcription

I watched his quill plunge – the feather
Appeared to have its own intelligence,
Speeding before his laggard fingers –
Line after line the letters flowed …
And then he stopped – as if the sentence
Had died from lack of ink. He croaked:

'But they that seek the Lord shall not want
Any good thing.'
                    He used to have this glow
When copying; but right now it was gone.

'Tell Baithéne to finish the rest,' he said,
And make it *beautiful*. Our work is holy.
We must ensure God's words are read –
The words I'll hear directly from His voice

Tomorrow on the grass of paradise.'

Last Words

I steadied him from chapel to his cell
And lowered him down on the floor
To gentle his head on his stone pillow.

I couldn't gather what he murmured,
A prayer, perhaps, I wasn't sure.

If I had known they'd be his final words
I might have flung questions at him
About angels, God, our brothers,
The greatest psalm? Or wept, said nothing ...

Instead I puzzled why he raised his voice
And humoured him: 'Be kind to one another.
That's all there is to life. Be at peace.'

Perhaps I thought I'd heard it all before;

But now it's all I think about – about it all.

Returning Home

As the midnight bell rang out
Columba hurried off to chapel,
Fearful that he might be late.

I was still quite far away
But could see the chapel windows
Full of a mysterious glow –

When I reached the door, the light
Vanished – plunging into blackness
As if blind I shouted out –

'Father, speak, where are you, father?' –
Stumbled through snares of dark,
Found him slumped beside the altar.

Other monks now running in,
Lamps ablaze, were wailing loud.
Then his eyes, now opening,

Shone, as if the monks were angels –
So I helped him lift his hand,
Give his blessing to the brethren;

Then he breathed his shortest breath …
Finally released his soul;
Yet his face had colour – not of death

But as reflecting heaven's gold.

Ernene in Donegal

The very night Columba
    Passed from earth to heaven
I was fishing with others
In the valley of the Finn
    And the raven-sheathed sky
Was suddenly illumined.

Towards the east a light –
    A pillar of fire – was rising
And flooding midnight
As if it were the sun at noon
    On a glorious summer's day;
Then the dark resumed.

Some other fishermen
    Had seen the valley lit
As by a thousand lanterns;
And all along the river
    Fish bobbled to the surface
Like coins of gold and silver.

About the author

James Harpur has published seven poetry collections and is a member of Aosdána, the Irish academy of the arts. His poetry is known for its explorations of spirituality and mysticism and he has won a number of awards. These include the UK National Poetry Competition, the Vincent Buckley Poetry Prize and a Patrick and Katherine Kavanagh Fellowship. His books include *The Gospel of Joseph of Arimathea* (2007), a 'journey into the mystery of Jesus'; *The White Silhouette* (2018), an *Irish Times* Book of the Year; *Angels and Harvesters* (2012) a PBS Recommendation; and *The Dark Age* (2007), winner of the Michael Hartnett Poetry Prize. He regularly broadcasts his work on radio and gives readings and talks about poetry, inspiration and the imagination in universities and schools and at literary festivals.

www.jamesharpur.com

Sources and acknowledgments

I would like to express my appreciation for all the scholars and St Columba enthusiasts of the past who helped me arrive at the poems in this book. They include, especially, Adomnán (d. 704), abbot of Iona, who produced *Vita Columbae*, the first and fullest account of Columba's life; and Manus O'Donnell (d. 1564), a scholar-chieftain, who produced, in Irish, *Betha Coluim Chille* ('Life of Columcille'), which incorporates material from various sources, including an older Irish *Life* of the saint. The translation work of modern scholars, especially Kuno Meyer, Kenneth H. Jackson and Gerald Murphy, has also been indispensable for versions from the Irish.

I'd like to thank Paul Ó Colmáin for his beautiful images, and everyone at Wild Goose Publications for their literary midwifery. A special thank-you to Professor John Carey for kindly answering various queries and John F. Deane for his wise guidance and encouragement; thanks, too, to Mel, Penelope and Evie.

Books consulted

Adomnán, *Life of Saint Columba*, trans. William Reeves (Lampeter: Llanerch, reprint, 1988); trans. Richard Sharpe (London: Penguin Books, 1995).

Carey, John, *King of Mysteries: Early Irish Religious Writings* (Dublin: Four Courts Press, 2000).

Carmichael, Alexander, *Carmina Gadelica* (Edinburgh: Floris Books, 1992).

Clancy, Thomas, and Márkus, Gilbert, *Iona: The Earliest Poetry of a Celtic Monastery* (Edinburgh: Edinburgh University Press, 1995).

Clarkson, Tim, *Columba: Pilgrim, Priest and Patron Saint* (Edinburgh: Birlinn, 2012).

Jackson, Kenneth H., *A Celtic Miscellany: Translations from the Celtic Literatures* (Harmondsworth: Penguin Books, 1971).

Meyer, Kuno, *Ancient Irish Poetry* (London: Constable, reprint, 1994).

Murphy, Gerald, *Early Irish Lyrics* (Dublin: Four Courts Press, 1998).

Ó Cróinín, Dáibhí, *Early Medieval Ireland, 400-1200* (Harlow: Longman, 1995)

O'Donnell, Manus, *Life of Columkille (Betha Colaim Chille)*, (1532), eds. A. O'Kelleher and G. Schoepperle (Urbana, Ill.: University of Illinois, 1918).

Waddell, Helen, *Mediaeval Latin Lyrics* (Harmondsworth: Penguin Books, 1952).

Sources for the poems

(NB: Reeves and Sharpe have a different numbering for Adomnán's *Life*. I have given Reeves first, then Sharpe in brackets.)

Part One: Exile

'Eithne's Carol': Adomnán, 3.2 (3.2).

'On Leaving Ireland': attrib. Columba; O'Donnell, p. 195, no. 192.

'Retrospect': attrib. Columba; Murphy, p. 65, no. 29; Meyer, p. 85; O'Donnell, p. 199, no. 201.

'Exile': from my sequence on Irish saints (in *The Dark Age*, 2007). The tradition that Columba settled in a place from where Ireland was invisible is found in Dr Thomas Garnett in his *Observations on a Tour through the Highlands* (1800), Vol. I, p. 248.

'Nostos': attrib. Columba; Murphy, p. 67, no. 30.

'Islands': attrib. Columba; excerpted from Jackson, p. 279, no. 222.

'Bountiful': attrib. Columba; Meyer, p. 86 (from 'Colum Cille's Greeting to Ireland'); O'Donnell, p. 285, no. 275.

'To Live in Derry': attrib. Columba; Meyer, p. 87 (from 'Colum Cille's Greeting to Ireland'); O'Donnell, p. 295, no. 279.

'The Oaks of Derry': attrib. Columba; Meyer, p. 87 (from 'Colum Cille's Greeting to Ireland').

'Nine Waves': O'Donnell, p. 191, no. 184.

'The Worst Fear': attrib. Columba; O'Donnell. p. 85, no. 89.

Part Two: The Mayhem of Miracles

'Wings': Adomnán, 1.29 (1.37).

'The Skull': O'Donnell, p. 129, no. 131.

'Vision': Adomnán, 1.1 (1.1).

'Columba the Scribe': attrib. Columba; Murphy p. 71. no. 33.

'The Oratory of Light': O'Donnell, p. 177, no. 168.

'The Missing Vowel': Adomnán, 1.17 (1.23).

'Spilled Ink': Adomnán, 1.19 (1.25).

'The Visitor': Adomnán, 1.35 (1.48); O'Donnell, p. 269, no. 265.

'Ballad of the Milk Vessel': Adomnán, 2.15 (2.16); O'Donnell, p. 301, no. 284.

'The Creature in the River Ness': Adomnán, 2.28 (2.27); O'Donnell, p. 307, no. 289.

'Psalm 44': Adomnán, 1.29 (1.37). NB: Brude is also known as Bridei.

'The Healing Stone': Adomnán, 1.1 (1.1).

'Ballad of the Spring': Adomnán, 2.9 (2.10).

'The Falling Monk': O'Donnell, p. 333, no. 309.

'Columba on the Island of Hinba': O'Donnell, p. 335. no. 311.

'Bread of Light': Adomnán, 3.18 (3.17).

'Defending the Poets': O'Donnell. pp. 353-355, no. 332.

'The Pattern of the Day': O'Donnell, p. 437, no. 398; 406.

'The Whale': Adomnán, 1.13 (1.19).

'Song the Contrary Winds': Adomnán, 2.14 (2.15); O'Donnell, p. 299, no. 283.

'Abbot Cainnech's Shoe': Adomnán, 2.12 (2.13).

'Baitan's Grave': Adomnán, 1.14 (1.20).

'O Apple Tree': Adomnán, 2.2 (2.2).

'The Door': Adomnán, 2.37 (2.36).

'Ballad of the Book of Glass': Adomnán, 3.6 (3.5); O'Donnell, p. 247, no. 243.

Part Three: Waiting for the Angels

'Harvest Spirit': Adomnán, 1.29 (1.37).

'Valediction of the Reptiles': Adomnán, 2.29 (2.28).

'On the Shore': O'Donnell, p. 441, no. 404.

'*Dies Irae*' (my translation from the Latin of verse 17 of the poem, *Altus Prosator*, traditionally believed to have been written by Columba): Waddell, pp. 78-79; Carey, pp. 44-45; Clancy and Márkus, pp. 50-51, 63.

'The Receiving Angels': Adomnán 3.23 (3.22).

'The Gift': Adomnán. 3.24 (3.23).

'The White Horse': Adomnán, 3.24; O'Donnell, p. 409, no. 361,

'Transcription': Adomnán, 3.24 (3.23).

'Last Words': Adomnán, 3.24 (3.23).

'Returning Home': Adomnán, 3.24 (3.23); O'Donnell, p. 413 ff., no. 363.

'Ernene in Donegal': Adomnán, 3.24 (3.23).